Wedding Wonders

Tales & Traditions,
Customs & Curiosities
by Kimberly Burton Allen

0 43422 69559 1

Cover Design and Typography by Roy Honegger

Published by Great Quotations Publishing Co., Glendale Heights, IL

Library of Congress Catalog Card Number: 96-76132

ISBN 1-56245-264-9

Printed in Hong Kong

ACKNOWLEDGEMENTS

I'd like to thank the following people who provided insight, resources, ideas and assistance: Marguerite Schondebare, Lyn Ross, Norma Weiss, Nancy Eng, Alison Cornish and Lisa Reynolds. Also, my sincere appreciation goes out to Father John of the Greek Orthodox Church of the Hamptons (Kimisis Tis Theotokou) and Rabbi Myron Kinberg of the Jewish Center of the Hamptons, who double-checked my research.

Most of all, I owe a debt of gratitude to my husband Chris, whose love and patience, forbearance and support makes all things possible.

INTRODUCTION

Congratulations — you're a bride!

Yes, you know that women have been marrying for millenniums, yet you feel…*special*. And you are! Those of us who've gone before thrill for you as you plan your big day. As a bride, you become part of a fabric which has been woven throughout the ages — of love between a man and a woman.

Whether you've planned a formal, white-tie-and-tails ceremony in a cathedral, or a shorts-and-swimsuit service on a sandy beach, you'll likely make certain traditions a part of your wedding. Perhaps these customs reflect your heritage or religious beliefs. Or perhaps they're purely sentimental—a way to pay homage to family or loved

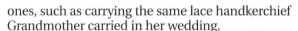

ones, such as carrying the same lace handkerchief Grandmother carried in her wedding.

The customs, traditions and superstitions found in this book reflect the cultures of many lands over thousands of years. Some are romantic, some are naive, but all are charming in the way they depict the beliefs of our predecessors. Whether you've incorporated many conventions or just a few, you create a wedding unlike any that has ever come before…a wonderful, personal experience that you'll remember always: the beginning of your lives together as husband and wife.

May your wedding day be filled with the love and best wishes of those who care for you, and may your future bring much happiness always.

— Kimberly Burton Allen

TABLE OF CONTENTS

Betrothal

The word wedding originates from the Anglo-Saxon *wedd*, meaning a pledge. Betrothed as children, a future bridegroom would ceremoniously place a ring on a young maiden's right hand as he gave her his wedd. The ring would be transferred to the left hand at the nuptials.

～

In olden days, a man "plighting his troth"
— from which the term "betrothal" was
derived — was entering into a legal
obligation which would only be validated
by the marriage.

~

The convention of a suitor asking a woman's father for her hand comes from the Roman ritual of *dextrarum junctio* — joining of right hands — where a father "handed over" his daughter to her new husband in marriage.

~

In many cultures, the "engagement" was simply an interval during which the bride-price or dowry could be agreed between the two families.

~

The ceremony of *engyesis*, which proclaimed a betrothal in ancient Greece, was essentially a wedding; legally, a marriage began the day of the betrothal.

～

A potential suitor in some parts of ancient Europe had to pay a woman's father a bride-price in order to wed. Before the use of cash, the bride-price generally consisted of property or an agreement that the groom-to-be would work for the father for a set period of time.

Bride-prices were established in Anglo-Saxon England after young men began to make a habit of stealing their brides. Unable in most cases to retrieve her before the marriage was consummated, the girl's family insisted on being reimbursed for the loss of a working member of the household.

~

When the bride-price set by her father was too high, a bride sometimes chose to run away with her suitor — from which the practice of eloping derived.

∼

Among many African tribes, a man cannot marry until he, his father or uncles have paid a brideswealth in money, livestock, or other valuables to the girl's family. This payment is an indication of the esteem in which they hold the bride, and the worth they place upon the new ties with her family.

In many cultures, the ancient custom of paying a bride-price eventually developed into a practice of settling a gift on the bride, so she could cover an unexpected emergency.

~

The traditional wording of wedding invitations, in which the bride's parents request one's presence at the marriage of their daughter to the bridegroom, evolved from the days when the bride was considered property that changed hands, from father to husband.

~

The dowry system, in which a bride was expected to bring valuables such as land, estate, or money into her marriage, was observed in many cultures. Originally a dowry was regarded as compensation for the burden undertaken by the new groom of supporting a wife.

Bridal showers date back to the days when a dowry was requisite to marriage. Their roots are found in an old Dutch tale that tells of a young miller in love with a maiden whose father, objecting to the match, withheld her dowry. Sympathetic villagers "showered" her with domestic goods until she had a large dowry, thus enabling the couple to wed.

Hope chests date back to the Middle Ages. Once made of wood by a father for his daughter, they were repositories of linens and other items collected over the years of her childhood, which she would need to set up her own home.

～

The father of a Greek bride betrothed his daughter in the fifth century B.C. by promising, in the presence of witnesses, to give her — and a specific dowry — in marriage, while clasping hands with her suitor or the suitor's father. This verbal, public oath was binding.

Women of the Zulu tribe of South Africa have long used a language of colored beads strung on necklaces in certain sequences to communicate wealth, ambition and disposition to potential suitors. White beads symbolize love and purity, black means marriage, green indicates jealousy, and red, anger. Yellow beads are impressive, for they tell suitors she can bring to a marriage much wealth in cattle.

In Ugandan tribes, a man wishing to marry goes to the potential bride's older brother and paternal uncle to negotiate a marriage. The young woman is summoned to the meeting and asked to pour beer. If she does so, it means she doesn't object to the bridegroom, and the bargaining proceeds without her.

Arranged marriages were, and still are, customary in many cultures. One practice among Hindus in India was to ask a bride under consideration to select a ball of earth from among four present, each taken from a different place. If she selected the ball made of earth taken from the cemetery, her suitor rejected her.

To win a bride, tribal societies, known for their intricate rituals of behavior, adopt a courting trait practiced by birds and other animals: Males adorn themselves with much color and ornamentation to attract the attention of a potential mate.

~

A Hindu dictum stated it was essential to his afterlife that a father arrange the marriage of his daughter before she was ten years old in order to attain a place in heaven. Were he to give her in marriage once she had reached puberty — when she was considered a mature woman — he would be condemned to hell.

Marriages among European Jews of the Middle Ages were commonly arranged through the use of a *shadchan*, or matchmaker, who worked for a fee. The matchmaker may have been a rabbi, but because communities were widely scattered and travel was difficult, the shadchan was often a travelling merchant.

An admirer in medieval Brittany proposed to the object of his affections by leaving a branch of hawthorne at her door on the first day of May. If she accepted his proposal, she left the branch; if she refused, she replaced it with a head of cauliflower.

~

To authenticate their engagement, a couple in medieval Brittany would intertwine their pinky fingers, close their fists, and drink from one glass, or cut bread with one knife. If she presented the knife to her fiance at a later time, it signified she wished to break the engagement.

~

Rings

The use of wedding rings is believed to have originated in ancient Egypt. Predating the coin, early Egyptian legal tender was called "ring-money," and was worn, ring-like. During a wedding ceremony, a groom placed a piece of ring-money on his bride's finger to signify that she was endowed with his wealth.

Centuries ago, it was proposed that even the exactness of a wedding ring's fit was symbolic — it exemplified the way in which a married couple should fit each other in taste, disposition and intellectual capability.

∾

That wedding rings are worn on the third finger of the left hand dates back to an ancient belief that the "ring" finger contained a nerve which went straight to the heart.

∼

According to romantics of the late eighteenth century, the wedding band's place on the third finger is metaphorical: While every other finger can be extended to its full length and straightness alone, the ring finger can only be fully extended in the company of an adjacent finger.

In Jewish law, in addition to a verbal declaration of marriage there must be an act of *kinyan* — a conferring of something of value upon the bride — for the marriage to be legal. A ring has been the preferred, traditional object of exchange since the seventh century.

~

The tradition of a diamond engagement ring dates back to 1477, when Archduke Maximilian of Austria proposed to Mary of Burgundy with a gold ring set with diamonds to form the letter M.

∾

Before the late eighteenth century, the scarcity of diamonds made their use in engagement and wedding rings an option available only to the rich. Coveted for their durability, diamonds became a symbol of indestructible love.

~

Historically, wedding rings were fashioned of gold and silver both for their value and their symbolism. Because gold was considered the most pure of metals, its use in a wedding ring brought to mind purity and honor, while rings forged of silver, the most musical of the precious metals, symbolized love's harmony.

Precious stones, each type attributed a special meaning by the Church of Rome, were popular in wedding rings in Tudor times. Diamonds were said to symbolize invincible faith; rubies, glory; sapphires, hope; emeralds, serenity and joy; onyx, sincerity; crystals, simplicity and purity; and amethysts, modesty.

~

An old French tradition, *regard rings*
became popular again in Victorian times.
The name "regard" is an acronym of the
gemstones used to spell out sentiments in a
ring: Ruby, Emerald, Garnet, Amethyst,
Ruby, Diamond.

First worn by the Irish in the early seventeenth century, *claddagh rings* feature two hands, symbolizing friendship, which hold a heart, meaning love, topped by a crown, signifying loyalty. It is worn as a wedding or betrothal ring when the tip of the heart points inward "towards the heart," or as a friendship ring when it points away.

≈

In the seventeenth and eighteenth centuries when jewel-encrusted "dress" rings became fashionable, the wedding ring evolved into a simple band, its purpose distinguished by its simplicity.

~

Once popular with sweethearts about to be separated for long periods of time, a *gimmal ring* was made of two or sometimes three loops which fit together into a single ring. Fashioned to each of the outer bands might be a tiny hand, which fit over a small heart on the central circle. The three parts

were separated at a betrothal ceremony and the couple each kept an outer loop while a witness retained the central one. When the marriage eventually took place the three segments were again united into one, which the bride then wore as a wedding ring.

∼

A popular style of wedding ring in
Elizabethan times was a *poesy ring*.
It was made up of two or three circlets
joined together, each hoop containing
an engraved line of a verse.

~

When to Wed

Marry when the year is new
  Always loving, kind and true.

When February birds do mate
  You may wed, nor dread your fate.

If you wed when March winds blow,
  Joy and sorrow both you'll know.

~

Marry in April when you can,
  Joy for maiden and for man.

Marry when June roses grow,
  Over land and sea you'll go.

~

Those who in July are wed,
  Must labor always for their bread.

Whoever wed in August be
  Many a change is sure to see.

Marry in September's shine
  Your living will be fair and fine.

~

If in October you do marry,
Love will come, but riches tarry.

If you wed in bleak November,
Only joys will come, remember.

When December snows fall fast
Marry, and true love will last.

~

An ancient Church prohibition against
weddings between Rogation (three days
before Ascension Day), and Pentecost (the
seventh Sunday after Easter), is thought to
be the reason an old folk rhyme that warns:
  Marry in the month of May,
  You will surely rue the day.

Ancient Roman superstition warned
against May weddings, believing that
during that month the souls of the dead
returned to intrude upon the living.

~

Roman maidens considered June to be
the most promising month to be married as
it was thought to be named after Juno,
goddess of love and marriage.

～

In ancient Greece, the most popular month for weddings was January. Called *Gamelion,* meaning "wedding month," it was believed to be a period of time blessed by the goddess Hera, who oversaw matters of marriage.

∼

Even the day on which one was wed held superstitious connections. Weddings on Monday, Tuesday and Wednesday were thought to bring far more luck than those held later in the week. Friday, especially Friday the thirteenth, was deemed a very unlucky day to be wed.

~

Whit Sunday, also known as *Pentecost,* is the most popular day for people to be married in Sweden.

~

Amish weddings are permitted only after
the harvest, and they generally take place
during the week, rather than on a weekend.

It was believed in some countries —
among them Scotland and Holland — that
the most auspicious time of day to marry
was during the rising of the tide, because
the ebb and flow of the tide symbolized
fortune and fertility.

~

Superstitions

Traditionally, a bride wears something old as a guarantee that the love and affection she enjoyed before her marriage will endure, something new for success in her new life, something borrowed as a symbol that friends may always be helpful when needed, and something blue to designate her loyalty and devotion to her groom.

Most wedding superstitions are based on the belief that the bride and groom need protection from evil spirits. One such protector was the best man, whose duties included making sure the groom didn't go back for anything once they had started for the church, as it boded ill for the marriage.

From the days of antiquity, the shape of the horseshoe has been thought to guard against evil. For this reason, English brides often stitch a tiny horseshoe into the lining of their gown for good luck, while an Irish bride might carry a silver horseshoe along with her bouquet.

~

An old Germanic folk belief says that men who hate cats will never find a wife, as cats were the favorite animal of Frija, goddess of love and fertility.

In Victorian times, the last thing a bride put on were her gloves, and to do so she would turn away from the mirror. It was considered unlucky for the bride to look at herself in the glass after she had finished dressing for her wedding.

~

One old superstition warned against a bride wearing pearls at her wedding, as pearls were thought to symbolize tears.

≈

An old wives' tale claims that a pinch of salt sprinkled in a bride's glove, pocket or shoe will guarantee her happiness.

It is considered good luck to give the
rabbi, priest or minister who officiates the
wedding an odd-numbered sum of money.

～

Long ago, a suitor did not propose to his intended bride himself, but sent instead a few friends to convey his request. On the journey, his representatives sought omens. If they came across a blind man, a pregnant woman, or a monk, it was considered a sign they should give up their mission, but a pigeon, a wolf, or a nanny goat was an indication of good fortune for the couple.

If a bridal party in medieval times came upon a snake, a rabbit, a dog, a lizard, a monk or a priest en route to the church, it was a bad omen for the marriage.

～

An old wives' tale in Wales advised a bride
to purchase something as soon as she
married, before the groom could buy
anything, for then she would be his
"master for life."

~

An old custom, observed in England and elsewhere, of placing a coin in the left shoe of the bride or groom was believed to bring prosperity, hence the tag on the old rhyme: "…something borrowed, something blue, and a sixpence in your shoe."

～

Ill-fortune is said to befall a bride who fails to remove and throw away every pin from her dress and veil when she changes out of her wedding costume.

It is considered good luck in England to encounter a chimney sweep, a black cat, a lamb, a toad, or a dove on one's wedding day, and a bride is especially lucky if she finds a spider in her wedding gown when she dresses. But hearing a cock crow after dawn, or seeing a pig or a funeral, is thought to be an ill omen.

In Switzerland and Holland, a pine tree is planted at the home of the new bride and groom to bring fertility and luck.

~

Before a Chinese bride leaves her house for her wedding, she dons a pair of her father's shoes and walks carefully from her room to the waiting bridal sedan while wearing them.

～

In Sweden, they say that if you pick a bouquet of seven or nine different varieties of flowers from an equal number of meadows on Midsummer Eve, and place the bouquet under your pillow, then you will dream of your bride or groom-to-be.

~

A Greek bride may tuck a lump of sugar
into one of her wedding gloves to bring
sweetness throughout her married life.

～

An old superstition warned: A bride who sneaks a taste of her wedding cake before it is cut will lose the love of her new groom. However, if she retains a bit of it after the wedding, she is guaranteed his faithfulness.

~

Preparing for the Wedding

On the day of the wedding, both bride and groom in ancient Athens would bathe in water from the spring of Kallachoran to ensure fruitfulness, especially in the production of an heir.

❧

The procession to an Elizabethan wedding was an event in its own right. Accompanied by an uproarious minstrel band, the bride and her party would be escorted by the groomsmen to the church where the bridegroom waited. Bystanders, finding this splendid entertainment, were likely to join the procession unless deterred by the groomsmen.

It is a rite in many cultures to convey the
bride secretly to the wedding ceremony.
In traditional Chinese custom, brides were
carried to the wedding site in a covered
sedan chair.

~

Elizabethan bridesmaids had much to do on the wedding day. After dressing the bride, they would tie flower garlands throughout the house where the feast would take place, strew rose petals and soft rushes on the path to the church, and make little "favor" bouquets for themselves to wear and guests to carry.

Before a tribal wedding in Kenya, special
artists are brought in to paint the bride's
hands and nails with an intricate series of
designs in henna, a blackish-red dye. The
stain remains on her hands for one year, to
display her newly-married rank in the society.

～

An strictly Orthodox Jewish bride will cut
her hair short before her wedding and wear
a *scheitel*, or wig, in public ever after. It is
believed only a husband should have the
liberty of seeing a woman's natural tresses.

~

In some parts of rural France where brides
lead a procession of villagers to the church,
it is traditional for village children to string
a length of white ribbon across her path,
which she must cut in order to pass.

~

In Slavic tradition, before a bride leaves her home for the church, her mother pours water over the step as a symbol that her old life has been washed away.

∼

Before contemporary printing processes, wedding invitations were engraved — the paper was stamped from below, producing raised letters which could then be inked. To prevent the ink from smearing, small rice-paper squares were placed over the printing. Though modern printing methods make it superfluous, tissues are still enclosed with many wedding invitations today.

Following an old custom, some Chinese brides give their grooms two symbolic gifts on the eve of their wedding: a wallet carrying a gold coin, to signify hope for wealth and prosperity, and a belt, that he remain bound to the marriage and faithful to her.

~

Regarded as a matrimonial rite in itself, an Iroquois Indian custom called for a bride and her mother to bring cakes made of maize to the mother of her future groom, who in return, would give them venison.

The Wedding
Costume

Used more than two thousand years ago, bridal veils considerably predate the wedding dress. They were yellow in ancient Greece and flame-colored in Rome. A Roman bridal veil cloaked the bride from head to foot, and was later used as her burial shroud.

~

A Roman bride dressed her long hair into six locks woven with ribbons, over which she wore a wreath made of flowers and sacred herbs. Atop the wreath flowed a long, red-orange veil, which was believed to ward off evil spirits.

~

Anglo-Saxon brides used their hair as a veil, and hid their faces completely behind a curtain of long tresses. A similar custom is still practiced in parts of Africa, where as an expression of modesty, some brides braid their hair into a veil that screens their faces.

~

In traditional Jewish weddings, a veil is a symbol of modesty, recalling the incident described in Genesis where Rebekah "took the veil and covered herself" when she first saw Isaac, her future husband.

~

Early Christian brides wore veils from the time of their betrothal until the end of the wedding ceremony.

~

An Oriental Jewish bride's veil is opaque. She must be led by hand to the *chuppah*, a canopy where the ceremony takes place. Her veil symbolizes complete trust and, quite literally, blind faith in her bridegroom.

～

A brooch has been the most common item of jewelry worn by a bride since Elizabethan times. Known as a "brooch of innocence," in Victorian times it was thought to symbolize purity. A more common belief, especially in the East, is that it was a talisman used to defy evil spirits.

~

Originally a crown made of olive or myrtle
branches, a garland was used to celebrate the
"royalty" of the bridal couple and is thought
to be the oldest part of the bridal costume.

~

A peasant bride in the Middle Ages wore a narrow circlet as a crown, under which she wore her hair loose or braided down her back as a token of her virginity.

~

It is customary in parts of Scandinavia for the bride to wear a *Vasa crown* — an intricate, bejeweled coronet — to symbolize innocence.

∼

The custom of the bride and her bridesmaids dressing alike evolved from an ancient belief that by doing so, evil spirits in attendance would be confused and therefore, unable to spoil a wedding.

~

Before white wedding dresses became customary, the color of the dress was thought by the superstitious to play an important role in the bride's happiness:

Married in white, you have chosen aright
Married in green, ashamed to be seen
Married in blue, love ever true

Married in pink, of you he'll aye think
Married in grey, you will go far away
Married in red, you will wish yourself dead
Married in yellow, ashamed of your fellow
Married in black, you will wish yourself back.

~

The color blue, thought to symbolize the virtue and innocence of first love, has been associated with weddings far longer than bridal white.

∼

Though Greek brides have worn white
since ancient times, white wedding dresses
and all their accouterments did not become
popular until 1840, when Queen Victoria
wore a simple white silk gown and a
matching veiled bonnet at her wedding.

~

Before Victorian times, special wedding dresses were seldom used; even the wealthy considered it an unjustifiable extravagance to buy a garment for one day's use. Brides simply wore the best dress they had, adding perhaps a special touch of blue.

~

Although bridal white originally was a sign of affluence during Victorian times, an era preoccupied with feminine purity and chastity, it became more symbolic of the bride's innocence. Indeed, white wedding gowns are often reminiscent of First Holy Communion dresses.

~

Wedding dresses of the second half of the nineteenth century were often two-piece ensembles consisting of a skirt and a bodice. While the bodice was frequently packed away as a keepsake, many a wedding skirt was later made into a christening dress worn by each successive child.

The morning of the wedding, Elizabethan bridesmaids would tie "love knots" of colored ribbon and stitch them all over the bride's dress. The knots represented the marriage bond, while the colors symbolized various aspects of fortune and virtue.

∼

In ancient Rome, after helping her daughter into her wedding tunic, the mother of the bride secured a woolen belt round the girl's waist with a "knot of Hercules" that only the groom could untie.

~

The favorite wedding dress of brides in the Middle Ages was one of vivid red, magnificently embellished. Costumes worn by bridegrooms were as resplendent as those of their brides.

~

Among Jews, the wearing of white is symbolic not only of virginity, but also of spiritual purity. In Orthodox practice, a white bridal gown is a declaration that in preparation for her wedding, the bride has been to *mikvah*, the ritual bath. Her groom wears a short white linen robe called a *kittel* belted over his suit to indicate his spiritual preparedness for matrimony.

Sephardic Jewish brides often wear
vibrant, colorful dresses and veils decorated
with gold coins closer in style to nearby
Muslim brides than to the white, Christian-
influenced wedding gowns of their
Ashkenazic sisters.

~

A Muslim groom is dressed in white and wears a special hat called a *kula*, while his bride often wears a red bridal robe shot through with gold threads and, per Islamic custom, is heavily veiled so that her groom does not see her face until after the ceremony.

∼

In Muslim custom, a mixture of henna leaves and water called *mehndi* is used to paint intricate designs on the hands of both the bride and groom on their wedding day to bring good fortune.

❧

Indian and Nepalese brides wear red saris woven with gold threads and, frequently, gold dust on their skin. In some parts of India, both bride and groom complete their wedding outfits by donning a robe made entirely of flowers.

∼

A Japanese bride wears a special, highly elaborate white wedding kimono during the wedding ceremony, and the traditional *tsuno-kakushi*, a white headpiece believed to hide "the horns of jealousy." During the course of the celebration, it is not unusual for her to change two or more times into other costumes, one of which may be a Western-style white wedding dress.

Traditional Chinese brides wear red,
which symbolizes joy and love. White,
denoting hope, is usually worn at funerals.

∼

The traditional wedding costume of a Navaho Indian bride is a dress woven in four colors, symbolic of the four directions of the compass: Black represents the north; blue, the south; white, the east; and orange, the west.

~

In eighteenth century England, men sometimes wore satin bows on their lapels, a custom descended from the wedding "favors" once made of ribbon, or flowers and ribbon, and given to guests. Today, men in Western-style weddings often wear a single flower as a boutonniere.

~

In traditional Chinese and Japanese weddings, the bride will change her costume several times during the day. She begins the day dressed in white, the color of mourning, because leaving her childhood home is symbolic of her death to her family. After her wedding, her home will be with her husband's people, and her true family will be his family.

Bouquets

The tradition of the bride's bouquet may have started with the Saracens and was later brought to Europe by the returning crusaders. Saracen brides carried sprigs of orange blossoms because the evergreen orange tree symbolized eternal love and fertility. Today, orange blossoms connote happiness and good luck.

~

A Roman bride carried ears of wheat, and later corn, as supplication to the gods that her husband's grain bins would always be full. By the time of the Renaissance, these stalks had been reduced to a sheaf; by the eighteenth century, a bouquet of flowers had become the practice.

～

Many brides in Tudor England carried bouquets of gilded marigolds dipped in rosewater, then ate the flowers after the ceremony. Marigolds were thought to be an aphrodisiac.

~

A tradition often observed in Britain is to tie knots on the end of the ribbons which adorn the bridal bouquet. The "lover's knots" represent the couple's unity, and each knot a wish for their good fortune.

～

The custom of tossing the bridal bouquet is thought to have originated in France in the 1300's. Tradition has it that if an unmarried woman catches the bouquet, she will be the next to marry.

～

Bouquets in Sweden often include
lavender, thyme or other piquant herbs,
reminiscent of early days when the strong
aromas were believed to ward off evil spirits.

≈

An American bride in the 1800's would toss a small bouquet to each of her bridesmaids. In one of them, a ring would be hidden, and the lucky maiden who caught it was thought to be the next to marry.

❧

The Ceremony

The term "to tie the knot" is thought to have originated from a practice in old Danish wedding ceremonies in which two pieces of ribbon were intertwined, to signify the joining of two persons into one.

⁓

Before he can be united with his bride, it is a tradition in Burma that the groom must pay money to her family and friends, then break through a barricade made of cloth.

～

Only since late medieval times has the blessing of a rabbi or priest been necessary for a marriage. For most of the Middle Ages, both Christians and Jews believed that through public articulation of vows and the bestowal of a wedding ring, a couple who wished to wed could marry themselves.

A Navaho Indian wedding ceremony takes place with the bride and groom facing east, the direction of the future.

≈

The African-American custom of "jumping the broom," symbolizing the start of creating a home together, dates back to the days of slavery. Couples would jump over a broomstick to the beat of the talking drum to demonstrate the leap into married life.

Both the man and the woman are crowned during wedding ceremonies in Greek Orthodox churches. This symbolizes that in the kingdom of the home, each must reign in his or her own realm and together share the joys and trials of married life.

～

The core of a wedding in ancient Greece was the *ekdosis*, which was a ceremonial procession of the bride from her father's house to that of her new husband. There she was formally given away to the groom.

~

In Roman times, a wedding ceremony might consist simply of the joining of the bride's and groom's hands in the presence of a number of witnesses. It wasn't necessary for the couple to live together for the marriage to be legal; often they did not.

∼

In Christian ceremonies, the bride stands on the groom's left — a reminder of the days of marriage by capture, when the man needed his sword hand free for defense.

~

The Quaker wedding is the simplest of all Christian ceremonies, usually taking place in an unadorned Meeting House without music, sermon, or special dress. Because Quakers believe that God, not man, makes a couple man and wife, a bride and groom generally proclaim their commitment to each other without the assistance of a minister or bridal attendants.

~

In England today, a special license, approved by the Archbishop of Canterbury, is required of anyone — including royalty — who wishes to marry in St. Paul's Cathedral, Westminster Abbey, or the chapel at Buckingham Palace, as none of these famous houses of worship are registered for the purpose of conducting marriages.

In Anglo-Saxon wedding ceremonies, the bride's father presented his new son-in-law with one of her shoes as an emblem of the transfer of authority. The groom completed the ritual by tapping his new wife lightly on her forehead so she felt the change.

≈

In Russian Orthodox wedding ceremonies, the priest holds crowns over the heads of the bride and groom as he recites the service. The couple drinks three times from a single "cup of experience" to symbolize their wish to fuse their lives into one.

～

Adorned in a turban and veil, a Hindu groom in India arrives at his wedding site leading a brass band, and sometimes dancers, to entertain the onlookers.

≈

The most important rite of a Hindu wedding ceremony is the Seven Steps — the bride and groom either take seven steps around the fire or circle it seven times, to represent blessings for food, strength, wealth, fortune, children, happy seasons and friendships.

The Celebration

The word "bridal" originated in medieval England as a by-product of the notorious drunkenness of their wedding feasts. The drink of choice was *ealu*, or ale, and so much of it was drunk in the bride's honor that the celebration became known as the *brid-ealu*, or "bride ale."

A contemporary version of the ribbon favor is a satin rosebud containing birdseed. The birdseed is thrown at the wedding couple as they leave the celebration, and the satin folded back up into a flower as a keepsake for the guest.

~

The basis of the wedding cake goes back to Roman times, when the ceremony included the bride and groom sharing a simple cake made of wheat flour, salt and water. Sharing the cake symbolized the couple's new unity.

~

Oatcakes, the traditional wedding cake in old Scotland, were broken over the head of the bride during the wedding feast. This was thought to aid the consummation of the marriage, and subsequently, the birth of children.

~

The first tiered wedding cake is credited to a baker in London who is said to have duplicated the shape of spires of a nearby church named St. Bride's.

∼

By Victorian times, bits of wedding cake had assumed the charm of matchmaking. A popular superstition said if you put a piece of wedding cake under your pillow and dreamed of the same man for three consecutive nights, he would be your future husband.

~

In some Victorian weddings, the wrapping on the slices of "groom's cake" would go so far as to list three eligible gentlemen of the lady's acquaintance. Upon awakening, the lady would open the paper to see if she had dreamed of one of the gentlemen listed.

～

One tradition that continued into Edwardian times was to bake a ring in the ingredients of the wedding cake. Guests were invited to cut the cake in turn, and whoever held the knife when the ring was exposed could be sure of happiness over the next year.

∾

According to a custom still practiced today, a bride must cut the first slice of her wedding cake herself. Her happiness and prosperity will be cut into otherwise.

~

A wedding cake custom popular in England is to eat the bottom tier of the cake at the reception, send the next tier out in small boxes to absent friends, and save the top tier for the christening of the first child.

~

The practice of tossing the bride's garter to the unmarried men is derived from a long-ago rough-and-tumble practice where young men wrestled the garter from the bride before the amused onlookers. The ritual evolved to where the bride herself distributed garters to her male guests, as a indication of her desire to lose her virginity through marriage.

Afterward

In a lighthearted ritual continued in parts of America until the late eighteenth century, a group of the bride's rejected admirers would kidnap her after the ceremony. To recover his wife, the new groom had to give her captors supper.

∾

One interpretation of the term "honeymoon" originates from the Teutonic custom of drinking a concoction of honey for thirty days — a moon's age — after a nuptial feast. Atilla the Hun is said to have celebrated his marriage so enthusiastically that he drank himself to death on his wedding night.

Some say the concept of a honeymoon period stems from the German practice of *flitterwochen*, literally, "tinsel weeks," a time of newness and radiance which, like the waning moon, eventually subsides. Therefore, it was believed the newlyweds should have a time to enjoy the passion and freshness of married life by themselves.

In ancient times, when marriage by capture was not uncommon, the Best Man's role was to aid the suitor in kidnapping his bride, then guard their hiding place from the often-wrathful family of the captured woman until the marriage was consummated (and thus irreversible). From this custom the modern honeymoon is said to have been derived.

When the bride at an Elizabethan wedding feast indicated she was ready to retire, groomsmen and guests would try to untie the "love knots" of ribbon, created by the bridesmaids, which adorned her dress. Superstition said that untying the knots would ease the pain of childbirth.

The custom of carrying the bride over the threshold dates back to Roman times, when it was believed that good and evil spirits resided at the home's entrance. If you stepped in right foot first, good would rule, but evil would prevail were you to enter on your left foot. Roman grooms, rather than risking that their emotional brides might be inattentive, carried them into the house.

On the day after her wedding, a Kgatla bride in southern Africa traditionally helps the women in her husband's family sweep the courtyard clean, to demonstrate that she recognizes and accepts responsibility to assist in the household duties until the newlyweds move to their own home.

～

OTHER TITLES BY GREAT QUOTATIONS

201 Best Things Ever Said
A Lifetime Of Love
A Light Heart Lives Long
A Teacher Is Better Than Two Books
The ABC's Of Parenting
As A Cat Thinketh
The Best Of Friends
The Birthday Astrologer
Cheatnotes On Life
Chicken Soup
Dear Mr. President
Don't Deliberate…Litigate
Fantastic Father, Dependable Dad
For Mother—A Bouquet Of Sentiments
Global Wisdom
Golden Years, Golden Words
Grandma, I Love You
Growing Up In Toyland
Happiness Is Found Along The Way
Heal The World
Hollywords
Hooked On Golf
I'm Not Over The Hill
In Celebration Of Women
Inspirations—Compelling Food For Thought

Interior Design For Idiots
Let's Talk Decorating
Life's Simple Pleasures
Money For Nothing, Tips For Free
Motivating Quotes For Motivated People
Mrs. Aesop's Fables
Mrs. Murphy's Laws
Mrs. Webster's Dictionary
Mrs. Webster's Guide To Business
Parenting 101
Real Estate Agents And Their
    Dirty Little Tricks
Reflections
Romantic Rhapsody
The Secret Language Of Men
The Secret Language Of Women
Some Things Never Change
The Sports Page
Stress Or Sanity
TeenAge Of Insanity
Thanks From The Heart
Things You'll Learn, If You Live
    Long Enough
Wedding Wonders
Women On Men

GREAT QUOTATIONS PUBLISHING COMPANY

1967 Quincy Court
Glendale Heights, IL 60139-2045
Phone (630) 582-2800
Fax (630) 582-2813